# *Sunsets*



*ISBN 978-1-5272-8876-8*

***My sincere thanks to Gail Parsons for her support and the beautiful illustrations that accompany each poem and bring them to life.***

*INDEX*

# *INTRODUCTION*

*This is my second short work of poems inspired and written during the period of grief for my late wife Sue following her death from cancer in St. Julia's Hospice, Hayle, Cornwall on 6th November 2019. Sunsets always stimulate vivid memories of Sue and the special moments we shared.*

*Bereavement is not easy and is unique to every individual and family who experience the grief. Thousands and thousands of us travel with the grief and manage the days with memories and reflection for those we love but now gone.*

*I have kept Sue's love and memory alive in poetry and illustration, although I am not a natural poet by any stretch of the imagination. My hope is that following touching comments about my first publication, "Reflections" readers may find comfort and inspiration during a difficult time. To discover there can still be more to life.*

*Keith*

# *Memories . . . . .*

*Walking a coastal path,*
*Sharing the delight of islands we love,*
*Fighting our way through dense Bracken,*
*Appreciating a mirrored lake,*
*The darkness of a canal tunnel,*
*Hand in hand on a beach,*
*You make them perfect.*

***Burgh Island, Bigbury on Sea, Devon. Memories of May 2003***

# *Hell Bay*

***"Brilliant today", said the walker in passing,***
***Yet, am I walking a path of loneliness?***
***This path we had trodden so many times,***
***A path of sand and sea grass, the sun at my back,***
***My face set towards Hell Bay and the turbulent sea,***
***Rock stacks casting shadows of autumn long,***
***Vivid images across the years still strong,***
***I feel your presence within sharing the memories,***
***You walk beside me, there is no loneliness,***
***So I build a column of granite stones,***
***A permanent shrine to our everlasting love.***

***Hell Bay is on the west coast of Bryher, Isles of Scilly.***
***The poem was written at the cairn, 17th October 2020.***

Pennine Way
FP Hawes

# *Path in Life*

***I recall that moment on the Pennine Way,***
***The magic of the Yorkshire Dales,***
***What can I make of this life?***
***I lift my eyes to the hills,***
***Where does my help come from?***
***My help comes from the Lord,***
***The Maker of Heaven and Earth,***
***He will watch over my life,***
***Watch over my coming and going,***
***Both now and forever more.***

***The Pennine Way near Hawes, September 2018***
***Poem is inspired by Psalm. 121***

# *I See the Wind*

*I see the rolling clouds and sheeting rain,*
*I see the silver wave through grass in a meadow,*
*I see a spray plume whipped up from the curl of a wave,*
*I see the resistant bend of a willow tree,*
*I see the nod of late summer corn,*
*I see the swirling vortex of autumn leaves,*
*I see the sway of your delicate white rose,*
*I lie in bed, listen to the boom and rush in the eaves,*
*I feel your presence tingle my face,*
*I recall the image of your flowing hair,*
*Like all these things*
*Tossed and blown by the wind.*

Stained glass window

Abbey Church

# *Spiritual Island*

*Across a stretch of blue sea,*
*The memories remain of that shared day,*
*When we held hands in that sacred Abbey church,*
*When we embraced in the Watchtower chapel,*
*Sunlight streaming through the leaded window,*
*Illuminating the marked text at the bible table . . .*
*"God so loved the world, that he gave His only Son . . ."*
*It gave an everlasting bond in that spiritual place,*
*Prayerful images of that special, peaceful, Caldey Island.*

*Caldey Island Cistercian Monastery is off the coast at Tenby, and can be reached by public boat.*
*June 2016.*

# *The Years of Our Lives*

*The setting sun a red ball across Mount's Bay,*
*An evening drifting to fading Light,*
*The gentle lap of waves on the shore,*
*A sense that you are all around,*
*Encompassing my spirit and my soul,*
*Embracing the days, the years, of our lives,*
*So we remember . . . .*

***Sunset across Mount's Bay, looking towards Newlyn and Mousehole.***

# *Light and Life This New Year*

***January blues, when the nights are dark and cold,***
***February with glowing fires, sunlight glistening from snow,***
***We look towards the light of the New Year,***
***Searching for a path to light and life,***
***Not looking back to where love's years have gone,***
***We're going to find true love this New Year.***

***Don't want to depend on love that's here then gone,***
***The intense light of Spring will take away the doubt,***
***Want to give this soul a feeling of love so alive,***
***We must depend on love that's here to stay,***
***There is light at the end of the tunnel,***
***God loves you more than you can say, this New Year.***

# *Finding Myself*

*I sit by the sea on a beaten rock,*
*I watch the ebb and flow of the surf,*
*In the suck of the wave trough*
*I recall those dear to me, now gone.*

*Many times in this life I have been cast adrift,*
*Some part of me is lost with each passing,*
*Love's years have gone along with part of my soul,*
*Feeling lost I have not understood all this.*

*Yet despite all, something within me is found,*
*I think the God of this world knows all,*
*Each day reveals a new aspect of life,*
*A grounding in new relationships, a realisation of being,*
*Once lost but now truly found.*

***St. Michael's Mount, Marazion, Cornwall***

# *Destiny*

***Sensing your life was slipping away,***
***Like sand through my fingers,***
***I wanted to keep you within my arms,***
***Moments shared in the shadow of your pain,***
***Wanting our love to last forever.***

***I felt helpless that I could not change our Destiny,***
***A Destiny that is beyond this earthly coil,***
***Yet love will endure,***
***Long after the sand has trickled away,***
***This experience of Destiny is a gift.***

# *The Shadow of Love*

*I walk with your shadow at my side,*
*The distinctive shadow that casts your love,*
*And follow a way like that of a pilgrim,*
*My pilgrimage to gather your love with every step,*
*Embracing the image of your smile, your flowing hair,*
*These thoughts fill my mind, permeate my soul,*
*You remain the core of my life,*
*I walk with your shadow as my hope and inspiration.*

***Thoughts of a snowy Vienna, December 2010.***

# This Burden of Love

*What do I make of my life,*
*Hold my head with my hands to my knees,*
*I try not to breathe, feel the burden,*
*These whirling thoughts that consume me,*
*I hold this burden within my breath,*
*Not just thinking about myself,*
*I remember everything you said,*
*Recall everything we did, over and over,*
*This burden is about intense love.*

# *Love's Years*

*Where have love's years gone?*
*It seems as if I have said goodbye to love,*
*But there are myriad of special memories*
*Yet these memories I cannot share,*
*And though I am surrounded by sincere words of comfort*
*The path is still one of sadness.*

*Must I live my life alone,*
*Things of unimportance magnified,*
*Each day trying to breathe in your spirit,*
*The spirit of your love to empower me,*
*I feel your presence burn within,*
*Can it be that your love will set me free?*

# *Eternal Flame*

***Spikes of melted wax on wrought iron,***
***The image of your candle flickers in my mind,***
***The candle that I lit privately***
***In hope that June day,***
***Lit that God might ease your pain,***
***A flame amongst many in the Abbey chancel,***
***Yet your candle is intense in my thoughts,***
***Burnt into my soul with reverence for the Spirit,***
***A spirit that brings me closer to you.***

***Votive candle lit in prayer for Sue***
***Tewkesbury Abbey, 20th June 2019***

# *Ebb and Flow*

*Inhaling the salty breeze in awe*
*Dazzling blue of sky mirrored in the sea*
*Granite rock stack towering through foam*
*The precise arc of a spiralling wave*
*Intense sunlight flashing and sparkling*
*The roar of breaking rollers, the rasp on sand*
*Debris and flotsam caressing the tide line*
*The ebb and flow of the sea.*

*The crackle and sparks of a driftwood fire*
*White smoke floats over rocks and boulders*
*The upper shore line dark in contrast to white sand*
*We embrace, hold close,*
*The towering cliffs a dramatic backdrop*
*In the sensation of the murmuring sea*
*We reflect on our identity through footprints in the sand*
*The ebb and flow of life.*

***Footprints in the sand, Durdle Door, Dorset. January 2001.***

GEP

# *Living in a Home by the Sea*

***So many years ago***
***From Skara Brae to the Brough of Birsay,***
***This ancient land has witnessed***
***Peoples, settlers and invaders***
***For thousands of years before Christ,***
***Living in homes by the sea.***

***An archipelago of causeways and tidal inlets***
***Spits of land forming islets,***
***Attracting inhabitants to toil and farm,***
***To evolve history on tiny island Holms***
***None more so than The Holm of Grimbister,***
***Living in a home by the sea.***

***The Holm of Grimbister, Orkney. Tidal Causeway. Population: 3.***
***We visited Orkney in 2015, but not Grimbister.***
***It was on Sue's list for next time . . . . .***